The Fruitful Bough

— Affirming Biblical Manhood

Study Guide

Warren Henderson

All Scripture quotations from the King James
Version of the Bible unless otherwise noted.

The Fruitful Bough – Affirming Biblical
Manhood (Study Guide)
By Warren Henderson
Copyright © 2008

Published by Warren A. Henderson
P.O. Box 416
Colfax, WI 54730

Cover Design by Heidi Spragg
Cover Picture by Massimo Gravili

ISBN 978-0-9795387-5-9

ORDERING INFORMATION:
Gospel Folio Press
Phone: 1-905-835-9166
E-mail: order@gospelfolio.com
Also available through various internet
book-retailers.

Printed in the United States of America

Table of Contents

LESSON #1 – *THE FIRST MARRIAGE* 1

LESSON #2 – *MARITAL COMPANIONSHIP* 3

LESSON #3 – *TO MARRY OR NOT?* 5

LESSON #4 – *MARITAL SATISFACTION* 7

LESSON #5 – *THE PERPETUAL PROBLEM* 11

LESSON #6 – *ASSISTING YOUR VINE TO CLING* 13

LESSON #7 – *COMMUNION AMONG THE CLUSTERS* 15

LESSON #8 – *ENJOYING THE FLOURISHING VINE* 17

LESSON #9 – *GOD'S CHOSEN LEADER* 19

LESSON #10 – *SHEPHERDING LESSONS FROM GENESIS (PART 1)* 21

LESSON #11 – *SHEPHERDING LESSONS FROM GENESIS (PART 2)* 23

LESSON #12 – *TOOLS OF THE SHEPHERD* 25

LESSON #13 – *SHEPHERDING TO THE GOOD SHEPHERD* 27

LESSON #14 – *MINISTRY OPPORTUNITIES* 29

LESSON #15 – *THE PORTRAIT OF A GODLY MAN* 31

LESSON #16 – *A CALL TO PURITY* 33

Notes

Lesson #1 – *The First Marriage*

Origin of Marriage

1. Did God initiate marriage or did man (Gen. 2:23-24)?

2. Given your answer in question 1, whose rules and desires should apply to marriage (Matt. 19:5-6)?

3. Does God's character and attributes change (Mal. 3:6; Heb. 13:8)?

4. Is man's behavior and character prone to change (Prov. 24:21; Jas. 4:14; Eccl. 6)?

5. What marriage problems would then develop if man's rules for marriage were applied instead of God's design?

Purpose of Marriage

1. What was God's primary purpose for marriage (Gen. 2:18)?

2. God designed the husband-wife relationship to be completely intimate (completely intertwined in all aspects).
   a. How was this design witnessed in the first marriage (Gen. 2:25)?

   b. Are we more or less vulnerable when open and revealed before others?

   c. How can we overcome vulnerability in our marriage?

   d. How can you assist your wife to move beyond chitchat to disclose her inner feelings more freely (Prov. 20:5)?

Purpose of Marriage (cont.)

3. God's secondary purpose for marriage is what (Mal. 2:15)?

A New Person Relationship

4. Marriage is a commitment to become a new person (becoming the right person vs. finding the right person).

    a. Do you consider your spouse's interests before your own and to be as your own?

    b. Is your spouse your closest friend, other than the Lord?

    c. Do you have full self-disclosure with your spouse?

    d. Do you work to develop activities that you can enjoy with your wife or do you tend to do your own thing?

5. Even though two people enter into a one-person relationship through marriage, who must remain the first-love of each spouse for the marriage to thrive (Matt. 22:37; 10:35-39; Rev. 2:4-5).

Lesson #2 – *Marital Companionship*

The Obligation of Marriage

1. Review from last chapter: Based on God's "purpose for marriage" what is the basic obligation in a marriage?

2. Understanding what companionship means: Use a Hebrew dictionary or determine from the book's text the meanings of the word "companion" or "partner" (speaking of the marriage partner) in the following passages:
   a. Prov. 2:16-17:

   b. Mal. 2:14:

3. Conclusion: Marriage is a relationship in which there must be constant _____ and _____ to thrive.

4. Review your marriage vows (or typical marriage vows if you do not remember yours).
   a. Did you make promises to "give to" or "take from" your spouse?

   b. Are these promises conditional or unconditional?

   c. Was there any bargaining or conditions placed on you in giving to your spouse?

   d. Did you agree to receive anything?

   e. Are you obligated to God to give to wife even if she is not demonstrating love to you?

5. Is the foundation of marriage romantic or obligational love?

6. Do you have a mindset of pleasing your spouse in all matters and before satisfying your own desires?

The Fruitful Bough Teacher's Guide

The Obligation of Marriage (cont.)

7. A commitment to good communication is essential for biblical championship to develop. Answer each of the following questions with a "yes," or a "no" and evaluate what effect you believe your communication habits (whether profitable or not) have on your wife's interaction with you?

   a. Do you have a habit of interrupting your wife while she is speaking to you, perhaps to tell her what she is going to say or to complete what you think she should say?

   b. Do you tend to engage in problem solving before your wife has a chance to express her frustration over a situation which has upset her?

   c. Do you generally avoid extended eye-contact with your wife when speaking privately?

   d. Do you usually provide non-verbal gestures while your wife is communicating with you to demonstrate to her that you are listening to and care about what she is saying?

   e. Do you usually ask non-interrupting questions to ensure you have understood what your wife has said or to get more information?

8. If your answer to the previous question showed some deficient communication skills, what changes do you plan to pursue in order to improve your interaction with your wife (remember you are under obligation to give to your spouse that which she needs in order to thrive in her God-given role)?

9. Although ignorance is often a factor, what one character trait often causes husbands to verbally mistreat their wives (Prov. 13:10, 29:23)?

The Commitment of Marriage

10. The Marriage Covenant:
    a. Who does a husband and wife make a marriage covenant with according to Proverbs 2:16-17?

    b. What occurs before God by the marriage covenant (Mal. 2:14)?

    c. How long does an unconditional covenant last (Ezek. 16:8; Matt. 19:6; 1 Cor. 7:39)?

11. Given the covenant imagery of Genesis 15:7-17 in which God is apart, how strong of a binding agreement does God consider a covenant made with Him to be?

Lesson #3 – *To Marry or Not?*

1. Besides companionship, what is God's general purpose for men and women (Mal. 2:14; 1 Tim. 5:14)?

2. Some men and women will not marry either by choice or lack of opportunity. What is one advantage of singleness (1 Cor. 7:31-32)?

3. What would be evidence that an individual does not have the wherewithal to remaining single (1 Cor. 7:1-2, 7-9)?

4. It is acknowledged in Scripture that some individuals will remain single for what purpose (Matt. 19:12; 1 Cor. 9:5-6)?

5. Explain what the meaning of Proverbs 18:22?

6. Though Adam felt loneliness, what was his physical condition just before God brought him his wife (Gen. 2:21)? Apply to your life (see also Ezek. 16:8).

7. Read the "Practical Guidelines for a Waiting-Single." Which of the guidelines do you believe you need to work harder on while waiting for direction in the matter of marriage? Be specific, what behavior patterns would you like to change?

8. If you do not feel like you are called to a single life, what areas of your life would you do well to improve while waiting for God's timing for marriage (e.g. practical skills, financial wherewithal, character qualities, bad bents, etc.)?

Lesson #4 – *Marital Satisfaction*

1. Read 1 Corinthians 13:4-8 and describe what biblical love is and is not (explain each aspect). Do you see anything interesting in the order in which these attributes are stated?

   <u>What love is:</u>   <u>What love is not:</u>

2. In which aspect of *what love is* (from your answer to question 1) do you need the most personal growth?

3. In which aspects of *what love is not* (from your answer to question 1) do you need the most personal change?

Recognizing Root Problems in Marriage (Part 1)

4. Poor communication (a couple must be able to talk together before they can walk together). What are some ways we can eliminate the sin which is blocking profitable communication?
   a. Eph. 4:25:

   b. Eph. 4:15; Col. 4:6:

   c. Prov. 10:19:

   d. Prov. 15:1:

   e. Eccl. 7:21:

Recognizing Root Problems in Marriage (Part 1 – cont.)

5. Mishandling anger.
   a. What happens if we internalize our angry feelings (Eph 4:26-27) and what should we do in such situations (Col. 3:13)?

   b. Should we resolve anger by venting rage at others (Eph 4:29-32; Ps. 37:7-8)?

   c. What are ways we can allow our anger to be used profitably (Prov. 27:17; Matt. 18:15; Eph. 4:15; 1 Cor. 10:31; 1 Pet. 2:19-24; Prov. 19:11)?

   d. What will eventually happen if we have close association with an angry person (Prov. 22:24, 29:22)?

   e. Generally speaking how fast should we get angry in everyday situations (Eccl. 7:9; Prov. 14:17, 16:32)?

6. Self-centeredness.
   a. Does the Bible ever "commanded" us to love ourselves?

   b. Who are we directed to unselfishly love (Mark 12:30, Eph 5:22-33, Titus 2:4, and Mark 12:3)?

7. Lack of Discipline.
   a. Are we born exhibiting disciplined behavior or foolish behavior (Prov. 22:15)?

   b. Besides obeying what is right and wrong per Scripture, what other behavior did the Lord Jesus often speak of as being desirable and undesirable (Matt. 7:24-27, 10:16, 24:42-46, also see Eph. 5:16)?

   c. How might a person be helped to learn disciplined behavior (Prov. 18:1; Gal. 6:2; Jas. 5:16)?

   d. If we are lacking discernment as to how to act, who should we seek (Prov. 20:5; 24:6; 27:5-6)?

   e. What area of your life do you lack disciple and what is your plan for correcting this behavior?

   f. In what ways is it evident to your wife that you value things or activities more than spending time with her?

8. Dealing with Sin.
   a. How does a believer recognize sinful living patterns (John 8:32, 16:13; 2 Tim. 3:16)?

   b. Once sinful living patterns are identified what should the Christian do (1 Jn. 1:9, 3:9; NKJV)?

8. Dealing with Sin (cont.).
   c. After awareness and repentance have occurred, what must a believer do to ensure that the sinful pattern does not return (Rom. 6:11-12, 13:14)?

   d. What the Word of God prohibits would be foolish to do and what the Word of God endorses would be wise to do, but what about those activities that fall into neither category (Phil. 2:12)?

Lesson #5 – *The Perpetual Problem*

Learning from the Past

1. Comment to the success and failures within Isaac and Rebekah's marriage as each followed or didn't fall biblical roles in marriage (also review Eph. 5:33):
   a. Their marriage was successful when Isaac _____ (Gen. 24:67)

      and Rebekah _____ (Gen. 24:63-65).

   b. Their marriage was unsuccessful when Isaac _____

      (Gen. 26:6-10; 27:1-4), and Rebekah _____ (Gen. 27:5-13).

2. Re-examine the list of "Dirty Fighting Strategies for Getting Your Own Way" presented in this chapter. List the five most common techniques you employ to manipulate your wife:

3. Do these behaviors promote or hinder good communication and problem resolution in a marriage?

4. How will you take corrective action for each of the five manipulative behaviors (be specific)?

Recognizing Root Problems in Christian Marriages (Part 2)

1. The Love of Money.
   a. What does 1 Tim. 6:10 say about the "love of money"?

   b. What often happens to those seeking to be rich (1 Tim. 6:9)?

   c. Who must we depend on for our needs (Phil. 4:4-6)?

   d. Where do riches come from and for what purpose are they given (1 Tim. 6:17-18)?

   e. What should a Christian do who is in lack (Phil. 4:11-13)?

   f. Describe with what a Christian should be content with (1 Tim. 6:6-8)?

2. Other Relationships. Describe how a married believer should relate to each of the following groups of people.
   a. Bad Companions (1 Cor. 15:33):

   b. Parents (Matt. 19:5):

   c. Neighbors ("Are we to keep up with the Jones?", 1 Tim. 6:6-11):

   d. In-Laws (Rom. 12:18):

   e. Business Associations (1 Cor. 5:9-10; Rom.12:2; 2 Cor. 6:14; Jas. 4:4):

   f. The Unrepentant (Rom. 16:17; 1 Cor. 5:11; 2 Thess. 3:6, 14):

3. Social Influences.
   a. The agenda of our social systems is controlled by whom (John 12:31, 14:30, 16:11)?

   b. What did Daniel say would happen in the later days according to Daniel 12:4 and how can this activity adversely affect home-life?

   c. Who controls what travels through the air waves and how can the media adversely affect home-life (Eph 2:2; 2 Cor. 11:14-15)?

   d. What is another degrading influence which can affect good home-life (2 Tim. 3:7)?

Lesson #6 – *Assisting Your Vine to Cling*

The Man's Roles in Marriage

1. Does God consider men and women as being humanly equal (1 Cor. 11:11; Gal. 3:28; Gen. 2:21)?

2. Is the husband or wife commanded by God to lead the family (Tit. 2:5; 1 Cor. 11:3; Col. 3:18; 1 Pet. 3:1; Eph. 5:23; Gen. 3:16)?

3. Explain in various ways a husband is to love his wife?
   a. Eph. 5:22-24:

   b. Eph. 5:25; Col. 3:19:

   c. Eph. 5:26-27:

   d. Eph. 5:28-29:

   e. Eph. 5:30:

4. Biblical love always starts by _____ (Eph. 5:25; John 3:16).

5. The Church's response to biblical love is to what (1 Jn. 4:19; Eph. 1:12)?

6. As a husband will you love your wife unselfishly?

The Fruitful Bough Teacher's Guide

The Man's Roles in Marriage (cont.)

7. What is the physical responsibility of the man to his family (1 Tim. 5:8)?

8. What is the spiritual responsibility of the man to his family (1 Tim. 2:11-12; 1 Cor. 14:34-35; Eph. 6:4)?

9. Example of man's accountability as family head.
    a. Who sinned first Adam or Eve (Gen. 3:1-6)?

    b. Who was held accountable for the sins of mankind (Rom. 5:12-21)?

Lesson #7 – Communion Among the Clusters

1. Read 1 Peter 3:7 and explain each of the following activities a husband is to engage in with his wife:
   a. "Dwell with them":

   b. "According to knowledge":

   c. "Give honor to the wife":

2. How well do your know your wife? Answer the following questions and then discuss the questions with your wife to confirm the accuracy of your answers (be sure to let her answer the questions first).
   a. What three things would your wife say she enjoys doing the most?

   b. What family-life matter would your wife say causes her the most anxiety or grieves her spirit?

   c. What would she say was your strongest character trait (speaking of behavior)?

   d. What behavioral bent in your life would she most like to see corrected?

   e. On a scale of one to ten (with ten being the best) how would she rate your marriage overall?

   f. If you have children, what would your wife say is her main concern with each child?

3. Read Matthew 6:21. Do you treasure your wife and if so is it in a way that she appreciates?

4. Review the following wrong ideas and attitudes discussed in previous chapters and evaluate yourself accordingly (rate your own behavior within your home-life on a scale of one to ten, with ten being the best score):

   a. I have a giving vs. getting attitude in my marriage.

   b. I pursue "new person" priorities in my marriage (i.e. seeking oneness and biblical companionship).

   c. I understand and seek to fulfill God's intended role for me as the head of my home.

   d. I love my wife sacrificially.

   e. I spend time listening to and learning about my wife.

   f. I am able to extend tenderness to my wife instead of bitterness.

   g. Christ is the center of our home or marriage.

   h. The Bible is the ultimate authority in our home for guiding family life.

   i. I am the spiritual leader in our home?

   j. I am the provider in our home?

   If you determine any of the above areas to be deficient jot down some new patterns of behavior that you would like to pursue to improve your marriage and home life.

Lesson #8 – *Enjoying the Flourishing Vine*

1. Review the portions of Song of Solomon quoted in this chapter. Characterize the expressions of these lovers towards one another and make an application to your own marriage.

2. Emotions strong influence a woman's sexual satisfaction. What can you do to cause better emotional disclosure with your wife and better prepare her for a romantic rendezvous?

3. Does Scripture reveal any details of the sexual relationship between the two lovers in Song of Solomon? What application can be made to your own marriage?

4. Why does Paul state that anyone committing fornication sins against his or her own body (1 Cor. 6:18)?

5. Explain the meaning of Hebrews 13:4.

6. Review the principles and commands presented in this chapter to guide honorable sexual conduct between a husband and wife. Evaluate your own marriage and identify changes that you believe are necessary to ensure a clear conscience before God. Do not write your answer down; just indicate in writing that you discussed this matter and your conclusions with your wife.

7. Given the counsel of 1 Corinthians 6:12-13 and Philippians 4:5, what sexual attitude should a husband be careful not to adopt with his wife?

Lesson #9 – *God's Chosen Leader*

1. Malachi 2:15 states that God wants "godly children" (not just children) to be the product of believing parents. Read Deuteronomy 6:5-9 and 11:18-21 and describe how godly children would be known.

2. In your opinion, what constitutes a Christian family?

3. If parents neglect teaching their children about the Lord and what He expects of them, what will likely happen (Judg. 3:1-2)?

4. What natural characteristic describes an untrained child (Prov. 22:15)?

5. What is the likely outcome of putting an untrained child in with a large group of other undisciplined children according to Proverbs 13:20 (this is a common practice in public education)?

6. Who is God's choice instrument for rearing up godly children to Him (Eph. 6:4; 2 Tim. 1:5, 3:15)?

7. There are several examples in the Bible and secular history of the generational consequences of good and bad parenting. Review Scripture and note an example of both.

8. Given your answer in question 7, which example do you want to follow in your home?

Lesson #10 – *Shepherding Lessons from Genesis (Part 1)*

Genesis 31:1-13

1. Jacob lived in a difficult family situation for years in regards to his relationship to Laban (Gen. 31:1-13). How can we apply Jacob's example of overcoming difficulties during this time period to our own personal situations?

Genesis 31:14-55

2. What wise action did Jacob take after God had instructed him to go back to Bethel?

3. What may happen if you act without discussing what you believe God's direction for your family is with your wife?

4. How do children spiritually benefit when they see their fathers always relying on God's Word family for direction and rendering decisions (Ps. 119:10, 105)?

The Fruitful Bough Teacher's Guide

Genesis 32:1-23

5. Though Jacob did not flee his troubles, what was his initial impulse when challenged with difficulties?

6. Rather than despair in family trials what are some good practices for fathers to do (John 14:1; 1 Thess. 5:16-18; 1 Pet. 1:13, 5:6-7)?

Genesis 32:24-32

7. Explain what the Lord wanted from Jacob and what Jacob wanted from the Lord and how they both received what each desired.

8. Men tend to rely on their own wisdom and strength during family crisis. How did the Lord teach Jacob to rest in Him during such times?

9. What two new things did Jacob receive during this encounter with the Lord?

Lesson #11 – *Shepherding Lessons from Genesis (Part 2)*

Genesis 22:1-11
1. How does Jacob's conversation with Esau demonstrate that Jacob understood his God-given responsibility to leading his family?

2. In various practically ways, many parents today are relinquishing their responsibility of raising their children for the Lord. List some examples.

Genesis 33:12-20
3. Jacob demonstrates a variety of shepherding skills in this portion of Scripture. Comment to each of the following skills and how you might better apply each to your own family situation.
   a. A good shepherd knows his sheep:

   b. A good shepherd leads softly:

   c. A good shepherd does not overdrive his sheep:

   d. A good shepherd does not allow others to lead his sheep:

4. Learning from Jacob's mistake, what are the consequences if family leaders do not consistently lead their families God-ward?

Genesis 34

5. If Jacob had taken better care of watching over his daughter Dinah what troubles could have been avoided?

6. As God created females to be responders to male initiation, from whom should daughters receive masculine affection until they are married?

7. When a Christian family or a member of a Christian family engages in sinful conduct that becomes publicly known what should be the family's first response?

Genesis 35:1-6

8. Jacob had not kept a close eye on his family and over time what had slipped into the home without his knowledge.

9. After God rebuked Jacob for this matter, what proper action did Jacob take?

10. Apply to your own family. What idols have snuck into your home: what is stealing the affection of your wife and children from the Lord? What action will you take to determine if there are idols in your home that you are unaware of?

11. Not only did Jacob's family remove their idols from the home, but they also gave up their earrings. Since God did not command this action why do you think it occurred?

12. Given your answer in question 11, what action might you do to ensure various things or activities never become a device which Satan can use to distract your family from spiritual thinking and their allegiance to Christ.

Lesson #12 – *Tools of the Shepherd*

1. Scripture identifies various tools that parents may use to train up godly children when used properly. Provide a short definition for each of the following parental tools and explain when this particular tool would be better to use than others for particular situations.
    a. Discipline:

    b. Instruction:

    c. Nurturing:

    d. Admonition:

    e. Exhortation:

    f. Encouragement:

    g. Rebuke:

    h. Correction:

    i. Conditioning:

    j. Counsel:

2. For each of the following situations, describe which parental tool(s) should be used to train the child and why (this assumes that you already have obtain the facts in each situation and are required to act). Note: Often combinations of tools are needed to accomplish the best result.
    a. For the first time, you witness your 5-year-old son secretly playing with matches in your garage.

b. Your 16-year-old daughter (who does not have a lot of driving experience) would like to drive to a winter retreat at a Christian camp, but there is a major snow storm predicted for the day she would like to travel.

c. Your 18-year-old son wants to study a particular field of study, which you believe is unprofitable as far as learning a valuable profession to provide for his family in the future.

d. Your 2 year-old-son has been repeatedly told not to climb the stairs in your home, but you caught him quietly sneaking up the stairs again.

e. Your seven-month-old has a habit of crying every time you put her into her crib to go to sleep. What should you do?

f. Your 18-month-old does not want to sit still or be quiet during Church meetings?

g. You have found out that your 14-year-old has snuck secular music into the house which you do not approve of.

h. There is a young man who seems to be trying to establish more than a friendship with your 17-year-old daughter.

Lesson #13 – *Shepherding to the Good Shepherd*

1. What is the most vital task that parents have concerning their children (Judg. 2:10-12; Mal. 2:14; Eph. 6:4)?

2. Given the dialogue between the Angel of the Lord and Manoah in Judges 13, what will be one of the most effective ways to teach children to pursue after God?

3. What practical application does Psalm 90:16 and 44:1 have for parents in the matter of ensuring God is know to their children?

4. If your children do not witness you engaging in regular prayer will they likely think prayer is necessary?

    a. How often do you pray with your children each day (not including at meal times)?

    b. How often do your children see you praying by yourself?

    c. How often do your children witness you and your wife praying together?

5. Do you have regular family devotions in which Scripture is used to teach and encourage your family (1 Cor. 14:34; Eph. 6:4)?

6. How do you encourage your children to consistently have their own "quiet times" with the Lord?

   a. Do you have daily quiet times with the Lord?

   b. If you are lacking in this area of fatherly leadership, what are some ideas for initiating these spiritual habits in your children's lives?

7. According to Psalm 119:11, why is the memorization of Scripture so important?

   a. Do your children have a Scripture memorization program (besides what might be administered by the Church)?

   b. Do your children witness you regularly memorizing Scripture?

Lesson #14 – *Ministry Opportunities*

1. Evaluate the word pictures of Genesis 49:22 and Psalm 128:3 and describe the location of fruit-bearing for both the fruitful bough (i.e. husband/father) and the fruitful vine (i.e. wife/mother).

2. What is God's creation order as defined in 1 Corinthians 11:3?

3. As indicated in Scripture, what is the difference in meaning between "image" and "likeness" (Gen. 1:26, 5:1-3; Heb. 1:3)?

4. Though Adam and his wife would have the same morally "likeness" (i.e. they acted like God would act) before choosing to sin, does Scripture speak of the woman being the image of God?

5. What three spheres of earthly authority is man to have leadership (Eph. 5:22; 1 Tim. 3:1-2, 2:12; 1 Pet. 2:17)?

6. If women are not to teach men (1 Tim. 2:11-12) or to publicly speak in the church (1 Cor. 14:34-35), what obvious role are men to have in the church and at home?

7. Read 1 Corinthians 11:7, 15 and describe who or what is the glory of God, the glory of man and the glory of the woman.

8. According to 1 Corinthians 11:3-16, what visible practice has God demanded in order to remind believers of His creation order?

Lesson #15 – *The Portrait of a Godly Man*

1. Describe the meanings of each of the following character traits which Scripture uses to identify a godly man.

   a. Blameless (Titus 1:6-7):

   b. Sober-minded (1 Tim. 3:2; Titus 2:6):

   c. Husband of One wife (1 Tim. 3:2):

   d. Not Greedy for Money (1 Tim. 3:3):

   e. Grave (1 Tim. 3:8):

   f. Temperate, Not Violent (1 Tim. 3:3):

   g. Tender and Sacrificial (Titus 2:2):

   h. Patient (Titus 2:6):

The Fruitful Bough Teacher's Guide

1. Describe the meanings of each of the following character traits which Scripture uses to identify a godly man (cont.).
    i. Sound Speech (Matt. 12:34; Jas. 1:27):

    j. Exhibits Spiritual Leadership (1 Cor. 14:34-35):

    k. Good Work Ethic (1 Tim. 5:9; Eph. 4:28):

    l. A Man of the Book (Titus 2:1; 2 Tim. 2:15):

    m. Contentment (Prov. 21:17):

2. All of us have character bents which need to be straightened. Of the above character traits, choose three which you believe need the most work to align your character with that of a spiritual man. If married, discuss these with your wife and ask her to hold you accountable on each of these areas of growth. Often we are not even aware of the way we behave, until someone calls our attention to it – this is where change begins.

Lesson #16 – *A Call to Purity*

1. According to Proverbs 7:21-22 what is the sexual sin of the man and the sexual sin of the woman?

2. How many of the five senses did the strange woman of Proverbs 7 use to lure the young man void of understanding to have sex with her (Proverbs 7:5, 10, 13, 17)?

3. What mistake did the young man of Proverbs 7 make according to verse 8?

4. Why did the young man of Proverbs 7 think he would not get caught (Prov. 7:9, 16, 19)?

5. Given your answers for questions 3 and 4, make some personal application which would help you guard against engaging in impure or immoral conduct?

The Fruitful Bough Teacher's Guide

6. Besides the command to abstain from fornication Paul summons believers to have a pure thought-life and speech concerning sexual misconduct. Describe what conduct Paul is referring to in Ephesians 5:3-5):

   a. Fornication:

   b. Uncleanness:

   c. Covetousness:

   d. Filthiness:

   f. Foolish Talking:

   e. Coarse Jesting:

7. Read Psalm 101:3; 1 Thessalonians 5:22, and Proverbs 23:7. Discuss the application of these verses in preventing a believer from engaging in sexual misconduct.

8. Contemplate Job's commitment to the Lord concerning his eyes (Job 31:1). Are you willing to make a purity pledge to the Lord? If not, what biblical reason would you have for not committing to holy living (1 Pet. 1:16)?

Notes

Notes

Notes

Notes

Notes

Notes

Notes

Notes

www.ingramcontent.com/pod-product-compliance
Lightning Source LLC
Chambersburg PA
CBHW081023040426
42444CB00014B/3325